k St John

r

Promoting Positive
Thinking

Also available:

The Emotional Literacy Handbook
Promoting Whole School Strategies
Antidote
1-84312-060-7

Nurturing Emotional Literacy
Peter Sharpe
1-85346-678-6

Unlocking Creativity
Robert Fisher and Mary Williams (eds)
1-84312-092-5

Thinking Skills and Problem-Solving
An Inclusive Approach
Belle Wallace, June Maker, Diane Cave and Simon Chandler
1-84312-107-7

Promoting Positive Thinking

Building children's self esteem, confidence and optimism

Glynis Hannell

 David Fulton Publishers

David Fulton Publishers
2 Park Square, Milton Park, Abingdon, Oxon OX14 4RN

270 Madison Avenue, New York, NY 10016

First published in Great Britain by David Fulton Publishers 2004

First published in Australia by Palmer Education Publishers 2004
Transferred to digital printing

David Fulton Publishers is an imprint of the Taylor & Francis Group, an informa business

British Library Cataloguing in Publication Data
A catalogue record for this book is available from the British Library.

ISBN 1 84312 257 X

Typeset by FiSH Books

Contents

Introduction

Understanding self-esteem, self-confidence and optimism

Self-esteem is your belief about who you ARE

High self-esteem	Low self-esteem
I am OK	*I am not much good*
I am the sort of kid other people like	*I feel a bit ashamed of myself*
Mostly I like myself a lot	*I do not really like myself much*

Self-confidence is your belief in what you can DO

High confidence	Low confidence
I am a great tennis player	*I am hopeless at maths*
I am a good reader	*I can't run fast*
I can make friends easily	*I say the wrong things*

Optimism is your belief that things will go well

High optimism	Low optimism (pessimism)
This is going to be great	*I'm going to hate this*
This will turn out really well	*This is going to end up really badly*
There won't be any real hassles	*There will be lots of problems*
I usually get lucky	*Things never seem to go right*

There are many children who are blessed with good self-esteem, high self-confidence and an optimistic view of life. *People like me; I'm a great tennis player; I usually get lucky.* These students will usually perform to the best of their ability, even in quite difficult circumstances.

Some students, however, have low self-esteem, low self-confidence and a pessimistic view of life. For them life seems hard and difficult and small hurdles become major barriers to success. *I don't like myself much; I'm hopeless at maths; Things never seem to go right for me.*

The qualities of self-esteem, self-confidence and optimism are not always stable. Just as even the strongest plant will wilt if left without light and water for too long, many children will lose esteem, confidence and optimism if their environment does not provide a positive growing environment for these important seedlings of a positive mental attitude.

Children's emotional growth can sometimes be a very tender plant. Sadly, psychological 'pollution' can stunt or even destroy what was previously healthy growth in the essentials of a happy approach to learning and life.

This book presents a teacher's guide to building self-esteem, self-confidence and optimism.

Chapter 1

Understanding High Self-esteem

Self-esteem is your sense of self-worth

Healthy self-esteem does not necessarily depend on appearance or on physical or intellectual capacities, although success in any of these areas certainly helps a lot. There are many children without exceptional talents who are blessed with a very strong sense of their own intrinsic value, not as performers or achievers but simply as kids in their family, students in their school and young people in their community.

Jake is a ten-year-old boy whose medical condition has limited his intellectual and physical development. He is struggling with his school work and cannot participate successfully in sport.

When asked how he does at school his standard reply is 'Pretty bad. I'm not smart, no way!'

But when he was asked who he would be if he could choose to be anyone in the world, his answer was: 'Anyone at all? I reckon I'd choose to be me...because my family wouldn't be the same without me...and my friends at school...they'd say it was weird...really weird...not having me around.'

Jake is a boy with low confidence in his intellectual and physical abilities but with strong self-esteem. He has a strong sense of his value as a person, at home and school, despite the fact that his contribution, in terms of school achievements, sporting trophies etc., is minimal.

A child like Jake, with a positive belief in his intrinsic value as a person, can grow into an adult who uses those capacities to the full, with a sense of purpose and satisfaction.

The characteristics of high self-esteem

Students with high self-esteem:

- value and respect their own unique set of characteristics;

- do not need to seek excessive reassurance from others about their personal approval rating;

- know that they do not have to be exactly the same as other people to be worth just as much as them;

- do not have to show off to prove that they are OK;

- have a sense of security, belonging and entitlement, in their home and their classroom;

- are reasonably resilient in the face of teasing because, whatever anyone says or does, they are comfortable about the sort of person they are;

- are not easily led, because they respect themselves and do not need to compromise their sense of right and wrong to please others;

- can accept praise without embarrassment or denial;

- can accept failure and criticism without undue distress;

- are not afraid to own up when they are wrong;

- are not ashamed to ask for help when they need it;

- can show respect to other people because they are secure in themselves;

- can accept blame and apologise when it is appropriate; and

- can win or lose with good grace.

Understanding low self-esteem

Low self-esteem is a sense of personal inadequacy

If a student does not really like themselves very much, then it may not matter how many prizes they win or how many times people tell them that they are great; they may still feel negative about themselves as individuals. An underlying sense of inadequacy can cast a very long shadow on the good things that happen.

Cassie is a confident A-grade student. She knows that she can do well in school. She is also a talented and very successful swimmer.

She, too, was asked to say who she would be if she could choose to be anyone else in the world. Her answer was: 'Oh, I'd like to be really famous and rich and everything and then people would think that I was really cool...and I'd buy them really good stuff and they'd want to come over to my place all the time.'

Even though she is such a talented and successful girl, Cassie's answer tells us that her self-esteem is probably not high. She does not believe that people like her for the person that she is, but could only like her for her prestige and her spending power.

Who knows what will happen to Cassie? We can guess that, however successful she is, she will experience a lot of heartache wishing for more, trying to capture the good feelings that accompany good self-esteem.

The characteristics of low self-esteem

Students with low self-esteem:

- may talk big to cover up their feelings of inadequacy;
- may run themselves down and never be satisfied with what they have done;
- are easily led because they need the approval of others;
- follow fads and fashions to try to fit in with the crowd;
- frequently look for attention and approval from others;
- think that expensive possessions will increase their personal approval rating;
- are easily upset by setbacks or difficulties;
- are easily upset by what other people say because they believe all the negatives;
- tend to blame their own mistakes on circumstances or other people;
- feel uncomfortable with praise;
- become overly defensive about criticism;
- are boastful or over-excited when they are successful;
- have trouble accepting defeat, become defensive and make excuses;
- show off to try to impress others; and
- expect to be rejected or set aside, so may try to get in first and reject others.

Buying your way to self-esteem

For some children with low self-esteem, having expensive possessions is the closest they can get to being an OK person.

'Other kids like me because I've got Playstation and I wear cool sneakers.

I know Mum loves me because she bought me a new mountain bike.

My teacher doesn't like me because I haven't got a computer.

The best time for me is when I get a new DVD.

Other people think that I am OK because my Mum and Dad have got two shops and a new car.

The good thing about me is that I have got two mobile phones.

The bad thing about me is that I have not got a TV in my room.'

Why do bright, capable children so often have low self-esteem?

Many bright children have surprisingly negative perceptions of themselves. Research shows that some children who are identified as especially bright sometimes do less well academically and psychologically than other children who, although equally bright, have just muddled along with the rest of the class.

How does this happen? The formal assessment of a child as having special talents can be an exciting and quite overwhelming experience for parents, grandparents and the students themselves. It is all too easy for the child to get the message that their value (to their family, their teacher, or themselves) is based purely on their capabilities and nothing else.

Certainly, they can *do* a lot of things well; but how much value would they have as a person if their 'performance' abilities were taken away? Bright children know only too well that capabilities can come and go. What if the next topic in maths really is too hard? What if they get second place in tomorrow's music competition? For a child who believes that their personal approval rating is based solely on their award-winning performances these are very scary possibilities.

Being identified as very bright can also mean that there is an unrealistically high level of expectation on the student to perform in an exceptional way, all day, every day. If your idea of who you are is so tightly bound up with what you can *do* that the two are inseperable, then high expectations (followed by the inevitable ups and downs of successes and setbacks) can erode your self-esteem day by day, like water dripping on a stone.

Happily, knowing that you are bright can also be very positive. One experiment simply asked children to imagine that they were smart and learn accordingly. Another experiment told teachers that particular children were especially bright (when they were not). In each of these situations the students performed better when they or their teachers thought that they were smart. The secret is to make sure that students first of all value themselves for who they are; then being bright comes as an additional and positive bonus.

> Melissa was one of the high-achieving students in her class. If she received a 19/20 for a maths test or a B+ for a project she is often tearful and distressed.
>
> 'It was so bad ... really bad ... and we had to call out our marks ... I felt so stupid ... I should have easily got 20/20 ... and I worked really hard on that project ... the teacher said it looked good before I handed it up ... and then I only got a B+ ... and he won't let me do it again.'

The high level of emotion that Melissa has invested in her performance tells us that her own personal approval rating is strongly connected to her academic performance. If she does well then she knows that she is an OK person, if she does poorly (her definition, not ours) then she is not an OK person.

She uses her scores as a benchmark for the day's 'exchange rate' on her value as a person. Yesterday, 100 per cent gave her a good exchange rate and she was temporarily happy; today the rate has fallen and she feels so bad, not only about her performance but also about herself. If she believes that she is only as good as her last test result, then that last result is going to carry a lot of weight.

What about students who do not have much success at school?

Doing well at school – academically, socially, in sport or in art – does of course make a substantial contribution to your sense of self-worth. But what happens to those students who are not destined to be high achievers in the traditional sense of the word?

Much will depend on how the student learns to view themselves in their school community. In turn, this will depend on what values the school community promotes. If the awards, newsletter congratulations and school assembly announcements only ever relate to academic achievements or sporting successes, then the less-able students may well feel that they are second-class citizens.

However, if the school community values personal attributes such as persistence, determination, compassion, good nature, energy, commitment, community spirit etc., then a much wider range of students will be seen as potential success stories.

Does being grouped together with other low-achieving students destroy self-esteem? It depends. Being in a regular class and feeling that you are simply not making the grade can erode not only your confidence but your sense of value as a person. Being identified as a 'dumb kid' in a special group is potentially equally damaging.

Wherever the student is placed it is vital that, within that group, the student has a chance to take responsibility, achieve success and see their own personal development flourish. It is true to say that the least-able students need the most capable and skilled teachers.

Similarly, if repeating a year is viewed, within the school community, as a clear indication that the student has 'flunked', then the experience can be a very damaging and negative one. This process is one that has to be thought through very carefully and handled with considerable sensitivity to protect the student's self-esteem.

Attempts to boost the self-esteem of low-achievers through the use of superficial rewards or praise can be especially problematic. Even the slowest child can recognise when they are being patronised. They can read the message that they are doing so poorly that adults have to make up good things to say about them. The Good Reader badge is an embarrassment to the student who knows that 'All of us thick kids get good reader badges.'

Building self-esteem at school

This can be difficult for the child to achieve on his/her own. If one teacher consistently behaves in a way that damages a child's self-esteem, the task of building it up again is very difficult for the next. The whole-school ethos should support the development of good self-esteem – for staff as well as pupils – and be understood by everyone in the school. The following headings may provide a useful policy outline:

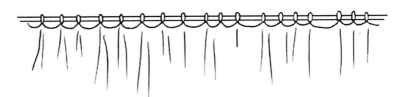

- Teach pupils to value individual differences and celebrate diversity.

- Value personal qualities as well as academic and sporting performance.

- Show trust and provide opportunities for responsibility.

- Show respect for the pupil when discipline is necessary.

- Show warm personal regard towards every pupil.

Teach the students to value individual differences and celebrate diversity

- Encourage students to understand themselves as unique individuals.

  I like to take time before I make a decision . . . my friend likes to decide quickly.

- Work on teamwork. Set group activities and discuss with the students how the team members brought different skills to the task.

  Ishmael had a great idea. Allana found just the right sort of stuff in the cupboard. Paddy was great at making it fun, etc.

- Avoid grouping students according to gender, seating position etc. when giving personal affirmations or rebukes.

  I am very disappointed with the boys . . . The blue table has done such a good job today.

  It is difficult for students to value their own individual worth if they are blamed (or praised) as part of an arbitrary group.

- Encourage the students to share their own cultural and family patterns to emphasise to the students that there are many, many ways of being part of a family, celebrating a birthday, spending the weekend, having fun or playing your part in your community.

- Ask your students to think about their class group as an ecosystem. What if the class was like a pine plantation or a sand dune, where every one is just the same? What is good about having a varied 'ecosystem' of people in the class group?

- Invite a parent or community member to talk to the students about their life's experiences and perhaps to demonstrate some of their unique skills.

- Remind students that they are unique.

  You're the best James Rigano I've ever met!

- Discourage any form of discrimination in your class. Teach your students that everyone has a unique value.

- Have a 'student of the week' and celebrate the diversity of students within your class.

  Tom is our student of the week, he is special because...we admire him for...

- Have a celebrity of the week. Encourage the students to choose a wide range of people. Discuss how personal qualities played a critical part in their success and fame: the Olympic athlete who showed extraordinary persistence and determination; the famous scientist who fought discrimination and persecution.

Value personal qualities as well as academic and sporting performance

- Give feedback about personal positives and not just academic abilities.

  You are really good at helping your friends...I can trust you...I like the way you kept trying with that.

- Have a classroom award that recognises personal qualities.

  Student of the day is Matthew for sharing his lunch with Zara.

- Ask the parents to write some affirming statements in their child's book.

  We're glad that Ali is in our family because...One special thing about Jasmine is that...I love it when Jack...one of the nicest things about Nathan is that...we love Dominic because he...

- Use stories and plays to explore the importance of personal qualities such as persistence, courage, kindness and honesty.

- Use the home-school book to communicate positives about each student's personal qualities.

  I'm sure you must be very proud of the way Aaron always plays fairly.

- Get the students to describe the positive personal qualities they notice in each other.

  I like the way Steve laughs a lot...Sara is very kind and friendly... Peter helps me when I can't find things.

Show trust and provide opportunities for responsibility

- Demonstrate trust. Ask: 'Now tell me your safety plans', rather than: 'Now I don't want anyone wandering off and getting lost.'

- Give responsibility and show trust: 'The drinks for the class picnic are being handled by Raymond and Shahira, so any questions speak to them – they know what's happening.'

Show respect for the student when discipline is necessary

- Use a reflective, problem-solving approach rather than accusations, yelling or blaming.

  We'll need to talk this through when we've all calmed down.

- Preserve the student's dignity.

  Jock you're a smart boy... you know that was the wrong thing to do... tell me some ways you can sort it out.

  Never use sarcasm, put-downs or ridicule.

- Give the student the opportunity to identify and solve a problem themselves to maintain their self-respect.

  I expect you can guess what I am going to say... now how do you think we should handle that... what would be a reasonable consequence to remind you not to do it again?

- Always speak courteously to even the youngest or worst-behaved student. If you have problems managing your own anger seek appropriate support. In the short term, ask someone else to deal with the situation.

- Only use natural consequences as punishments.

  You forgot the rule about respecting other people's right to work in peace... so for now you will need to sit by yourself.

  Never use punishments that only demean or humiliate.

- Only ever criticise the behaviour.

  I am disappointed that you behaved like that... you did the wrong thing just now.

Avoid criticising the student:

You are a big disappointment, Will Sparrow. You are an absolute menace, Bianca.

Show warm personal regard towards every student

- Take time to listen attentively, with good eye contact and true interest.

- Treasure what your students contribute to your professional life.

  Now, I want a really good photo of you all for my very own album . . . I'm going to write this down in my own journal – it's so special.

- Smile often at your students. Show that you are pleased to be with them.

- Greet each student by name and a warm personal greeting each morning.

- Share special times together and reminisce about them to build up a bond of shared experiences.

  I remember school camp . . . and Ben made us all laugh with his magic tricks.

- Avoid abbreviated names, pet names or nicknames unless you are certain that the student is comfortable about them.

Chapter 2

Understanding Self-confidence

Self-confidence is all to do with performance

In the previous section we looked the way self-esteem reflects the student's own self-portrait and how it can be nurtured by adults showing interest, care and respect. In general, self-esteem forms gradually. Although it can be damaged, serious harm usually only occurs when negatives have been extreme or persistent over a long period of time.

Whereas self-esteem is to do with the student's attitude towards themselves, confidence is all to do with performance. Because confidence is so closely linked to personal performance it can quite easily be destroyed in a moment. One slip from the tightrope, one really bad spelling test or one embarrassing comment from an adult can be all it takes to turn confidence on its head.

Self-confidence is variable

Self-confidence tends to be a much more superficial and variable quality than self-esteem. A student can be a confident reader and yet lose their nerve when they have to read out loud in front of the class. They can be a confident runner but a reluctant swimmer. A student can be full of confidence with one teacher, but uncertain and nervous with another.

Self-confidence develops through action

Confidence only develops through performance and action. You will never become confident about your ability to swim or read or do a science investigation unless you actually do it and feel pleased with how it went. The trick is to have enough confidence to take that first step, before you have had a chance to practise at all. We can all remember times when we have had to ride a bike, drive a car or stand in front of a class and teach for the first time. It helps if you can practise the skills in small steps, but sometimes the only way to begin is to 'take the plunge'.

Students vary in their confidence to try new and untried challenges. The confidence to 'have a go' is based on a general belief in your own capacities to cope with a new challenge and to learn quickly enough to avoid a disaster. This underlying confidence in yourself as a learner builds through previous experience of successful attempts.

Learning style and temperament

Underlying self-confidence is also part of our inborn personality and temperament. There are babies who are always willing to reach out, take risks and give things a try, and others who seem more cautious and unsure of themselves, taking time to gain confidence with any new skill.

Learning style also has an impact on a student's ability to demonstrate confidence with new things.

Students vary in the way they acquire new skills. Some children like to jump straight in and learn by trial and error, falling off their bike over and over again until they get the hang of riding it without taking a tumble. Other children prefer a watch-and-wait approach. They will stand by, watching, until they feel ready to give things a try. True, they will still need to go through a period of practice, but part of their learning has been through observation not action. While they have watched and waited they have been building up a mental picture of what they have to do and, with it, their confidence to take the first step.

Upbringing and environment

These factors will also play a very significant role in the development of self-confidence. Parents and teachers can make or break a child's confidence. If children constantly hear that they have already failed, are failing right now or are going to fail before long, then, inevitably, they will begin to assimilate this information. It is not only what we actually say but also what we imply that has such a strong impact on developing confidence.

Confidence builds through practice, and practice, inevitably, brings both successes and failures. As one child said when he was scolded for making an error: 'But I haven't finished practising it yet!'

Mark was asked to make a balsa wood boat for a homework assignment but his father insisted on making it for him, saying: 'It's hard to shape balsa wood for the first time...you could cut yourself...and it wouldn't turn out very well...you'd feel silly taking it to school...I'll do it and then you'll have a boat to be proud of...I bet it will be the best in the class.'

Mark's father really thought that he was doing him a favour by making him a really great boat to take to school. He had forgotten that confidence only comes through doing. Mark had had no chance to try out the new challenges of working with balsa wood. Mark has also had some very strong messages about his own capabilities: 'You're too stupid to even try to make a balsa wood boat...it would turn out badly for sure...and you'd cut yourself...you're so clumsy.'

Mark had even had a pretty strong message about life in general: 'It can be dangerous out there, even things that your teacher asks you to do can hurt you...it's safer not to try these things.'

Adults give out hundreds of messages about the value (or dangers) of trying new things. They also give out strong messages about what they believe about a child's abilities to try new things: 'Now you will be all right won't you?' (I don't think you are going to be OK); 'I'll be right here if you need me' (this is going to be so bad you're going to need me).

Confidence and motivation

Confidence has a very strong link with motivation. Generally speaking, motivation comes from the reasonable hope of success. The more confident you are, the more you are able to hope for success and the more motivated you will be.

One of the best ways of judging a student's confidence in themselves is to look at their willingness to perform a task or skill. A confident student will swing into action and tackle tasks that they believe they can attempt successfully.

However, if a student believes that a task is beyond their capabilities, they may try to avoid the task, be reluctant to start or fail to persevere. They may even refuse to do the task at all by becoming angry or tearful.

Those students who seem to be unwilling, non-compliant or just plain lazy are usually resisting learning because they simply lack the confidence to participate.

Confidence and anxiety

Confidence builds up through successful performance. However, self-confidence is stunted by anxiety about failing. If the student has a strong fear of failure then confidence will be battling against adverse conditions. If the student is relaxed and accepting about failures that occur in the practice stage of skill acquisition, then confidence will build up much more quickly. Anticipation of success and fear of failure can be two opposing forces in the process of building confidence. Keeping anxiety within bounds helps confidence to grow and flourish.

Ownership of success and failure

Some students do not take ownership of their own efforts and successes. They attribute success to luck or other people's efforts: 'It was really easy, the teacher told us how to do it.' These students may also blame their failures on bad fortune or other people's inadequacies: 'It wasn't my fault; I didn't hear what I had to do... It was a stupid question.'

Interestingly, there are some students who take the blame for their failures on their own shoulders but credit others for their successes!

Self-confidence will not build up if successes and failures are attributed to outside forces (good luck, bad luck, the teacher). If you believe that you won a race because at the time you were wearing a lucky medallion then your confidence in your running ability will be neutral.

Building confidence depends very much on the belief that you succeeded because you made it happen. If you believe this then you also believe that you can succeed in the future because, once again, you can make it happen.

Students' confidence often wavers when they make mistakes during the practice phase of learning new skills: 'If I've got it wrong then I'm no good at it.' Students need to understand that errors are a normal part of the learning process. They also need to discover that the mistakes they make are good sources of information about how to get things right.

Building self-confidence

Build confidence by showing confidence

- Focus your student's minds on the fact that they have the capacity to attempt the task.

  I know that you can give this a really good try... (rather than emphasising the student's ability to complete a task), *I know you can do this.*

- Confidence builds from believing that something is possible, so help your students by showing that you believe that they can do it. Give grounds for your confidence.

  This is just like the ones you did so well yesterday, so I know that you will be fine.

  Note: It is critically important that your expectations are realistic and not beyond the student's capability. Nothing destroys confidence like being set up for failure.

- Show confidence in the student as a reflective learner and ask them to evaluate their own work.

  Show me where you think you need to do some more editing...which parts are you pleased with?

- Make praise informative so that the student knows that you have grounds for your confidence in their ability. Instead of 'Good job' try:

  This really shows how much your spelling skills have improved – look how many words you've got 100 per cent correct.

Work with parents to build students' confidence

- Remind parents that the point of most classroom and homework tasks is to learn and consolidate skills and understanding, rather than to produce a piece of paper covered with correct answers or a perfect model boat. Give clear guidelines about the objectives of homework tasks: *Students will practise the skills involved in working with balsa wood; students will experience the novel process of designing, planning and making a model boat.*

- Remind parents that giving responsibility and trust is an important way of building self-confidence. Predicting failures *(I'll do this, it's too hard for you)* tells children that they have not earned the confidence of their parents. So why should they be confident in themselves? Rescuing children too often has much the same effect *(You forgot your swimming gear again. I'll rescue you because I know you are not clever at remembering)*.

- Show parents how to teach, not test, to build confidence in the student.

- Listen to parental concerns about their child's self-confidence. Some children disguise their lack of confidence in front of their peers and teachers.

Match tasks to the student's level of skill and learning style

- A task that is much too easy will not present any interest and will tend to reduce confidence *(She must think I'm really dumb if I've got to do this stuff)*.

- A task that is way too hard will overwhelm and defeat the student before he/she has started *(There is no way I can do this)*.

- A task that has a moderate degree of difficulty works best in engaging the student's interest. Success with tasks of moderate difficulty also brings the best sense of personal satisfaction *(Whew! That wasn't so easy, but I did it)*.

  A word of caution: 'moderate difficulty' is a very subjective thing. What a confident, capable child might think of as a reasonable challenge can easily be seen by a less-confident child as a huge and impossible challenge.

- Recognise that some students like to watch and learn before they begin active practice. Provide opportunities for the students to watch a skill or task being demonstrated. Enhance the students' learning by giving an explicit description of what is happening *(I am standing on the edge of the pool. I get my toes just over the edge, see? Now I am making sure that I am nicely balanced and comfortable)*.

- Give students practice time and ask them to nominate when they are ready to 'perform' *(Let me know when you are ready to read to me)*.

Match tasks to the level of the child's confidence

- If a child is very confident, then he/she will be able to cope with a fairly high degree of challenge without getting swamped.

- If a child has little confidence, then he/she is better off with a small challenge that looks manageable from the start.

- Allow the child to select his/her own level of difficulty. Provide various levels of scaffolding and let the student decide how hard they will make the task. *(This looks hard; I'll use the resource folder to get myself started and I will ask my buddy when I need help . . . This looks OK; I think I can do it without using the calculator).*

- Identify level of difficulty so that students can judge for themselves how they are going. Struggling and eventually succeeding with a task that has been identified as tough can build confidence; struggling with a task that you assume is supposed to be easy can destroy confidence.

Distinguish between 'getting it right' and 'doing it right'

- Many students get anxious about their ability to perform a particular task because they are not certain that they will achieve a perfect outcome. Always make sure that the students understand that it is often the journey and not the destination that makes for a successful exercise.

  The 'destination' of a task might be that the students will all have completed a project on the animals of Africa. The 'journey' will almost certainly involve time management, resource collection, collaborative learning, research skills, written and graphic communication, persistence, and many other academic and personal skills. Ensure that the students understand that their success will relate to the way they tackled their journey (they managed their time well, they worked well with others; they sought help when they needed it . . . they did their best with the skills and equipment they had).

- Base the criteria for success on personal, not group achievements. The concept of a 'personal best' works just as well in the classroom as in competitive sport. Just as sports men and women are warmly congratulated when they achieve a personal best, so, too, your students can celebrate their own personal best performances. A *Personal Best Achievement Board* in the classroom is a good way to acknowledge and record individual achievements.

● Encourage students to evaluate their own approach *(I was pleased that I found a good book in the library...I found making the index difficult...I need to find a better way of putting things in alphabetical order).*

● Mark students' work against the learning objectives so that they can see where they succeeded in '*doing* it right', even if they did not '*get* it right'.

● Ask the student to evaluate the outcome of the task in terms of its process *(How did you find that out...which parts did you enjoy doing...which parts did you find hard?).*

Success relates to the ways students tackle their journey

Teach new skills by structuring tasks and using guided learning

- Teach in stages and give demonstrations (this is especially important for students whose learning style is to learn first by watching and then by doing).

  - **Demonstration and explanation** *(See, first I put my ruler on the page, like this. I check that it's nice and straight and then I draw along the edge).*

  - **Modelled practice** *(Let's do it together. We'll put our rulers on the page. Let's check that they are straight... ready? Then let's draw along the edge of our rulers).*

  - **Guided practice** *(Now you do it by yourself. What's first?... that's good... now check... OK, off you go).*

  - **Monitored practice** *(You show me how you do it... it's looking good... fantastic!)*

- Subdivide a difficult task into small sections and teach one section at a time to build skills and confidence through practice and success.

- Teach skills by 'backward chaining'. This means that the student masters the stages of the task by working backwards from the finish. *(The student lacks confidence in swimming across the pool. She starts half-way across the pool so that she only has the final half to swim. Each day she takes a step back and swims a little further).*

- If the task is a big one, break it up into stages and celebrate reaching each stage. *(The task is to learn how to spell the 100 most commonly used words. To spell 25 correctly is a bronze achievement; 50 is a silver; 75 is gold and; 100 is diamond).*

- Encourage the student to set their own learning goals, monitor their progress and celebrate their success *(My goal is to learn to do this sort of multiplication by Friday. I will know that I can do it well when I can do 15 of them with no more than three errors).*

- Allow scope for errors in setting the benchmark for success. *(There are 20 questions. You need to get 15 or more right in the first set before you go on to the next set).*

Teach the students to use positive self-talk to build their confidence in themselves

- Negative self-talk disrupts performance and destroys confidence *(I'll never do this...I am going to fall over...this is too hard...I'll get it all wrong)*. Teach students to use positive self-talk *(I can give this a try...I know I can do this)*.

- A student can practise positive self-talk by acting as a coach for another student. It is always easier to be positive if someone else is taking the risk of failure! Ask the students to listen to their own coaching statements to their classmates *(You can do it...keep going...don't give up...you are getting there...it's not too hard...you can do it...just keep trying)*. Remind the students that they can be their own coach, using the same statements to coach themselves to success.

- Students can remind themselves of positive thinking by putting self-affirming slogans on their books, bags, desks or pinboards *(I can do it!...If I want to, I can...I'll give it my best shot)*.

- Encourage students to attribute successes appropriately. *(I did that well because I got started on time and put in effort; I can be confident in myself)*.

- Encourage students to attribute failures appropriately *(I did not do that well because I did not give myself enough time)*.

- Encourage students to realise that mistakes they have made need not be repeated *(Next time I will start earlier so that I have time to do it properly)*.

- Use stories, biographies and other resources to show students that extraordinary odds can be overcome through determination and confidence.

Build confidence by practising the task or skill

- Confidence is related to performance in a specific skill. It does not readily transfer from one skill area to another. You gain confidence in your swimming ability by practising your swimming. Do not expect to build your student's confidence in reading by, for example, giving them more practice in playing the drums.

- When teaching, it is important to make sure that students have enough opportunity to practise a skill. Many students (especially those who find learning hard) barely master one skill before they have to move on to the next. Just being able to scrape through a task, knowing that your mastery is very fragile, does not build confidence. Being able to do a task or demonstrate a skill with ease, because you have had sufficient practice, establishes a solid base of confidence.

- With difficult or complex tasks, teach and practise the subskills to start. For example, teach a child to draw circles and straight, curved and diagonal lines before teaching letter formation. Allow plenty of practice at each stage so that confidence builds up in steady increments.

Managing anxiety

- Ensure that students clearly understand that adults know that, as learners, their performance will be patchy, and that this is part of normal learning.

- Help students to analyse errors and mistakes as constructive pieces of information that will help them to improve their performance next time. *(Now, let's see what happened here...OK, you did the first bit just right...now we come to the bit you found tricky...mmmmm...look how you put this down here...where do you think it should go...?)*

Chapter 3

Optimism

Understanding optimism

Optimism is thinking and feeling, all mixed up together. The way we think has a very strong impact on the way we feel. The way we feel has a strong impact on the way we think. Thinking in a certain way produces feelings that match the situation: *(this is going to be awful...I feel scared...this is going to be great...I feel excited!).*

Emotion can also drive thinking: if we feel depressed then we think about things more negatively than if we are feeling happy: *(I feel so fed up...and this book is so boring...I'm so happy...everyone seems so nice today).*

Optimism is thinking positively

You can 'know' that things are probably going to work out well even if, as yet, you do not have all the facts. You can believe that whatever happens, you and others around you will find a way to solve the problems that occur. This is a form of intuitive positive thinking. It is enhanced by positive previous experiences. If, in the past, things have worked out fine, then in the future they probably will as well.

But, we find that optimists look at the past in quite a different way from pessimists. The optimist will think back: 'It was a shame that it rained at the picnic; still, we all had heaps of fun, the food was great and we all dried out eventually.' The pessimist will remember: 'It was awful the way the rain spoiled our picnic...we couldn't play outside, I fell over in the mud and I got cold and wet.'

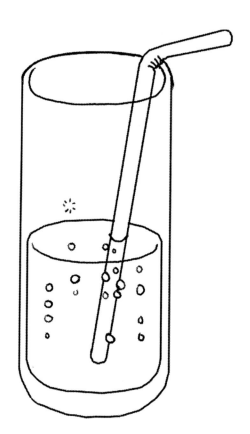

Is your glass half-empty or half-full?

The way we interpret past experiences colours the way we look forward to the future. The optimist will look forward to the next picnic – rain or shine, lots of fun, great food. The pessimist will look forward to the next picnic with trepidation: 'What if it rains? The picnic will be ruined again.'

The optimist will probably have an intuitive 'knowledge' that next time the weather will be fine: 'Don't worry, I'm certain it will be fine.' The pessimist has an equally strong intuitive 'knowledge' that it will rain again: 'I just know it, it will rain again just like last time... it's sure to rain.'

Pessimists tend to make a catastrophe out of a problem: 'It was really horrible... the other kids said really mean things to me... and they nearly beat me up... they nearly killed me... and Mrs Johnson didn't even care.' The optimist will keep things in perspective or even minimise what happened: 'Those other kids were pretty mean to me yesterday... I didn't care... I just ignored them.'

Optimists tend to feel that they have some control over what happens to them: 'I can ignore them... I can keep out of their way... I can choose to be upset or not.' Pessimists tend to feel that they are passive victims of circumstances: 'Those kids could have killed me and I could not have done anything to stop them... even my teacher didn't help me out.'

Optimism is feeling positive

Your emotional state can set the scene for the way you think. Emotionally, you can 'feel' positive and happy about the future, for no good reason, other than 'I feel happy now and I expect I will feel happy later on.' Of course, the reverse can also be true: 'I always feel fed up... and I bet I'll be just as fed up in the future.'

Pessimism, which is driven by emotion, is really part of depression. Children and adults who feel depressed think in a negative, pessimistic way, because that is how they feel. These emotions are driven not only by external events and internal thinking but also by biological factors that control our moods.

Trauma and optimism

Even the most positive optimist can have their positive belief systems and positive feelings knocked by an extreme trauma. When a tragic event occurs in a family, a community or the world, all children, optimistic or not, will feel and think negatively for a while: 'If our neighbour was mugged, then the world is more dangerous than I thought it was...I feel scared.' If the terrorists can bomb those people then maybe they will bomb us too.'

Optimists will probably recover more quickly than pessimists, but if a truly dreadful event occurs, all students, even the most optimistic, will need to find ways of rebuilding their positive expectations for the future.

Building optimism

Interpreting the past positively

- Help children to learn to interpret the past positively *(Remember that picnic...wasn't it fun when we all had to run to get out of the rain...what was the best bit of the picnic for you?)*.

- Help children to keep a sense of perspective about bad things that have happened that were a shame *(Was it a big problem or was it just a bit of a nuisance...did it still turn out OK in the end?)*.

- Use humour to translate bad experiences into positive ones *(I was so mad when I fell in the mud...you should have seen me...I looked like a chocolate donut!)*.

- Re-interpret events to show that what seems bad at the time does not necessarily predict how things will go in the future *(Remember when you didn't want to go to swimming club...look how you love it now)*.

Thinking ahead positively

- Encourage students to believe that they can have some control about how their future shapes up *(If you don't get chosen for the team this season you could try again next year)*.

- Encourage active, positive planning to make good things happen or to minimise problems *(I could take my cricket bat to school and ask that kid to play with me and my friends)*.

Dealing with trauma

● Take steps to protect children from the more dramatic images and reactions to the trauma. Children do not need to see TV news interviews with traumatised adults expressing their darkest fears, or to see death or destruction in graphic detail.

● Talk to children calmly and honestly about what has happened.

● Acknowledge that the child is entitled to feel frightened and insecure for the moment.

● Give a sense of perspective and distance *(It was a long long way from where we live...that was so sad that she died like that...but remember all the happy times she had).*

● Maintain the idea of a happy, safe world *(Yes, that was a terrible thing to have happened...but do you know that at the very same time, in other parts of the world, lovely things were still happening, just the same as ever).*

● Give the child something positive to do to express their feelings *(We could write them a little note to say how sorry we are...we could send some money to help those poor people).*

Recognising depression

Although many children with negative moods or negative thinking patterns respond very well to adults' efforts to change these and, with this, lighten their mood, there are some children who do suffer genuine, clinical depression.

Children and adults who feel depressed think in a negative, pessimistic way, because that is how they feel. These emotions are driven not only by external events and internal thinking, but also by biological factors that control our moods.

It is important to recognise when a student is clinically depressed. Some students may seem sad, withdrawn, low in energy and poorly motivated. Depressed students become agitated and angry. This must be discussed with the student's parents. Further professional advice is advised.

Optimism (and pessimism) can be very infectious. If children are surrounded by adults who are optimistic, it is likely that the children will share in the general mood of positive thinking. Similarly, negative thinking and pessimism can be very easily transmitted to children. This is particularly so because young children are often very literal and concrete in their understanding. Emotive words such as 'disaster', 'devastating', 'terrible' and 'threatened' can carry a lot of weight in a child's mind. As one eight-year-old said, 'and I am scared about the environment...how they are cutting down the trees and there's not enough water...soon there won't be enough food...so when I am a teenager I might have to die'.

- Encourage active, positive planning to make good things happen or to minimise problems: 'I could take my cricket bat to school and ask that kid to play with me and my friends'...'We could all be sensible about how much water we use'...'We could take our umbrellas and raincoats next time'.

- Use measured language to describe possible negatives: 'It will be a nuisance if we miss the train', rather than: 'It will be terrible if we miss the train'; 'we need to look after our environment'.

- Put negative information in context so that children understand the bigger picture.

- Model a positive, optimistic view of the future in what you say and do.

Create an environment that fosters happiness and optimism

- Use music and poetry to give your classroom a happy and optimistic outlook.

- Select (or create) a class theme song that is optimistic and affirmative. Sing it often.

- Allow plenty of time for activities that give children fun, laughter and joy.

- Use art and drama to add beauty and joy to your students' lives.

- Use stories, biographies and autobiographies to give children a sense of the strength of the human spirit.

- Preserve, nurture and share your students' inborn sense of wonder in our beautiful world.

Using Student Questionnaires

It may be useful to use these questionnaires to gain an impression of students' feelings of self-esteem, confidence and optimism when working intensively with them. The responses may also provide starting points for reflection and discussion.

Students will respond in very different ways, and great care is needed in interpreting their responses. It is important to remember that this is an informal screening and not a psychological assessment tool.

Some pupils will take the opportunity to express their feelings openly, and perhaps reveal significant problems. They may indicate that they feel that adults (parents/teachers) are disappointed in them. They may have a pessimistic view of life. Perhaps they are overly dependent on the possession of material items for their personal happiness.

Others might disguise their feelings and give very neutral, non-committal responses which do not correspond with your feeling that they have significant issues with confidence, self-esteem and optimism. In these circumstances, it will be important to follow up with further investigation and professional advice.

Students' responses should not be revealed to, or discussed with, fellow students. However, teachers will have a duty of care to discuss concerns with the student and/or parents/carers. In some situations, a counsellor may obtain prior permission from parents to give the pupil an assurance of confidentiality when the questionnaire is used as part of an ongoing counselling programme.

The two questionnaires which follow are not scored. They are completed by the student(s) to provide parents and teachers with some insight into the issues that may be impacting on self-esteem, self-confidence and optimism.

Photocopying of the questionnaires is permitted provided no changes are made and that each questionnaire is copied and used in its entirety.

A pupil questionnaire (1)

Complete the sentences below:

1. If you asked my mother what sort of a person I am she would say: ....

2. If you asked my father what sort of a person I am he would say: ....

3. If you asked my teachers what sort of a person I am they would say: ....

4. Other kids think I am: ....

5. I think that good things about me are: ....

6. If I could change the sort of person I was, I would like to be more: ....

7. If I could change the sort of person I was, I would like to be less: ....

8. If I could choose to be someone else I would choose to be............................... because they are: ....

9. People don't realise that I am: ....

10. I annoy people when I: ....

11. If I could choose how old I was I would like to be .... years old because:...

12. I am really good at:..

13. I am not very good at:..

A pupil questionnaire (2)

Circle YES, NO or MAYBE.

My mother thinks that I am a nice kid
to have around.   YES   NO   MAYBE

My father thinks that I am a nice kid
to have around.   YES   NO   MAYBE

My teachers are pleased that I am in
their class.   YES   NO   MAYBE

The other kids at school think that
I am OK.   YES   NO   MAYBE

Sometimes I think that I am not
good enough.   YES   NO   MAYBE

When I try something new I can
usually do it.   YES   NO   MAYBE

I think that in the future mostly
good things will happen to me.   YES   NO   MAYBE

I often worry about what might
happen to me.   YES   NO   MAYBE

Positive attribute cards

You can photocopy and enlarge these sheets many times, so you can make lots of cards to give to your students. It's a good idea to use special paper – bright colours look great, or you could decorate the cards with glitter. Write the student's name and the date on the reverse to personalise each card. Students love to take these special cards home. Some teachers give small rewards once students have received a certain number of cards.

I'm very impressed. You are listening so well

You are working very sensibly – I'm so pleased with you

You were a good friend to another student today – thank you

You remembered what you had to do without being reminded – great!

You've remembered the rules very well – fantastic!

You have been using excellent manners today – thank you

You took responsibility when you did something wrong – I'm pleased

You are really concentrating well – you're a top student!

I like the way you keep trying when things are tough

I noticed that you waited your turn today – thank you

You played fair and were a good sport today – well done!

I'm impressed. You kept your cool today – and did not get upset – well done!

You've got some really great ideas – good thinking!

You listened to what I wanted and did it straight away – great!

You are taking good care of your things – smart thinking!

You got started with your work quickly today – tremendous!

You did as you were asked right away – I'm very proud of you

I saw you stop and think and then you made a good choice

You listened to the warning and did the right thing – good thinking!

You are putting in a tremendous effort – that's great!

You are doing a fine job with your work – congratulations!

You owned up and told the truth – I'm proud of you

You are so good at ignoring distractions

You offered to help straight away – thank you

You ask really good questions – smart thinking!

I'm glad you said sorry when you made a mistake

Thank you for being so helpful in our class – you're a star!

You're so good at getting started with your work

Printed in the United Kingdom
by Lightning Source UK Ltd.
128588UK00006B/107-108/A